Water World
Children's voices

An educational booklet on water for children

Water World
Children's voices

An educational booklet on water for children

Published in December 2003.
© 2003 UNEP
ISBN: 92-807-2388-X
Produced by the Division of Environmental Policy Implementation (DEPI)
Director: Svein Tveitdal
Project coordinator: Nirmal Andrews
Project supervision at UNEP: Akpezi Ogbuigwe
Conceptualised by: Akpezi Ogbuigwe, Levis Kavagi and Clara Rudholm
Editorial advisor: David Simpson
Project administrators: Levis Kavagi, Clara Rudholm, Julia Washika and Wangari Kirumba
Peer review: DEWA: Salif Diop, Patrick Mmayi, Tessa Goverse
     DPDL: Halifa Drammeh, David Smith, Meryem Amar
     Dams/DEPI: Wanjiku Kaniaru
Layout design: Ideas a Monte, Portugal
Cover picture: Lo Wing Tung, Hong Kong
Illustrator: Ladislaus Regis Ondieki
Regional coordination: ROLAC: Gabriela Hoffmann
     ROA: Angele Luh
     ROAP: Timothy Higham, Jane Lugo, Tarawan Sarubudhi

The supervision of the layout and printing of this booklet was carried out by the Eco-Schools International Coordination (Foundation for Environmental Education). We acknowledge the contributions of Sérgio Santos and Sónia Sabino.

The DEPI team wishes to thank Mr. Eric Falt whose encouragement gave us wings to fly.

We also thank the following group of people who read through the manuscript and sent in very useful comments: Joseph Igbinedion, Barbara Jones, James Mwaniki, Ellen Schei Tveitdal, Faith B. Onyimbo and Jemaiyo Chabeda.

Thanks also to Catherine Steyberg for translating Spanish poems and essays into English.

我家附近有一条河涌，它与珠江相连。以前河里淌着从附近排出的污水甚至有动物的尸体，臭极啦，令人恶心。

最近，这条河涌开始进行整治，人们疏通河道，开设污水处理厂，为了改善周边的生态环境，人们还在河边种了许多花草树木。

如今，河涌里流动的水一天一天变干净了，偶尔还能见几条游动的小鱼，微风拂动，岸边花香，河边成了供我们散步的好地方。

Yao Momo, China

Drawings

Pictograms

 Poems

 Essays

 Activities

Questions

 Facts

Contents

This booklet captures the world of water from the eyes of children. It is written in the form of a story. The narrator, Nthabi, is a 14 year-old girl from Kenya, who teaches us about water, using her own experiences, along with pictures, poems and essays from her friends around the world.

I would like to thank all the children who have provided material for this book, as well as their teachers and all those who encouraged and assisted them to think about what water means to them. I would also like to acknowledge the Foundation for Environmental Education and UNEP's regional offices for supporting and coordinating this project.

This is one of a growing number of UNEP TUNZA products and activities to educate children and involve them in environmental decision making. TUNZA, the name of UNEP's children and youth strategy, means 'to treat with care and affection' in the Kiswahili language of Kenya. UNEP children and youth publications include *TUNZA: Acting for a Better World, Pachamama: Our Earth, Our Future*, and *TUNZA*, the UNEP magazine for youth. Every two years UNEP organizes the TUNZA International Children's Conference on the Environment.

I hope you enjoy reading this book and learning about water, our most precious resource. If you want to find out more about water, or about UNEP's activities for children and youth, please look at our web site *www.unep.org*.

Klaus Toepfer
Executive Director
United Nations Environment Programme

"WATER - TWO BILLION PEOPLE ARE DYING FOR IT!"

"Water - our life giver" means we cannot live without water. Only three percent of the water in our planet is freshwater for consumption, the rest is salt water. We must use water very carefully without wasting and polluting it because water is extensively used in our daily lives. Agriculture and industry as well as other living things like plants and animals require water.

At present, we see that man is wasting water by opening taps for a long time, when brushing teeth or when talking with each other while the bucket overflows with water. On the roads we see leaking taps and broken pipes not repaired for many weeks.

In history we are told that ancient Kings of Sri Lanka built large tanks or reservoirs to manage water. They built large tanks to collect water during the rainy season. From these tanks water was sent through canals to irrigate the fields. Further, deep wells were dug to conserve groundwater resources.

Harvesting rainwater is another new method of water management. Domestic rainwater harvesting where rainfall is collected from roof run offs into storage tanks after filtering is becoming very popular in many countries. We have to conserve water because without water there will be no life on Earth. Let us follow the words of King Parakramabahu, an ancient King of Sri Lanka.

"Let not a drop of water that falls from the skies flow to the sea without it being used for the benefit of man."

Lakshika Chamini Weragoda, Sri Lanka

One of the children who contributed to this booklet

WATER

Two Billion People are dying for it.

Welcome to Water World!

Chapter 1

Welcome to Water World!

Hi and welcome to Water World! My name is Nthabi. I am a 14-year-old girl and I live in Kenya, in East Africa. I welcome you to share with me some of the important lessons about water.

I will also tell you some of my secrets, and show you some letters and stories from my friends, just like the one you can find in the beginning of the book. My friends come from all over the world. I will tell you more about them and how we got to know each other later. Just like you and me, they are very interested in knowing more about water and, of course, the best way of doing so is to share with each other what we already know!

While reading this book, you will come across essays, poems, paintings and drawings. It is my friends who have sent them to me.

So, now I think it is time for us to start the journey into the wonderful world of water!

Nthabi

Lo Wing Tung, Hong Kong

The role of water
in our everyday life

Water is life!

Chapter 2

Water is life!

I am sure that most of you already know how important water is for all living creatures in our world. We all need water to survive - you, me, my friend Sasha, the trees in the forest and the birds in the sky. As our friend George from Uganda writes in the poem below, Water is life!

WATER IS LIFE

Water! Water! Water is life
People can't eat without you
Animal can't eat without you
Birds can't eat without you
Snakes can't eat without you

Water! Water! Water is life
Two billion people are dying for you
Billions are fighting for you
Billions are dirty
Billions are thirsty

Water! Water! Water is life
Children need water
Mothers need water
Elders need water
Sick people need water

Water! Water! Water is life
Birds sing for water
Animals bark for water
People cry for water
Snakes hiss for water

Water! Water! Water is life
Fish can't live without you
Plants can't live without you
Animals can't live without you
Rich or poor can't live without you

Onen George William, Bishop Angelo Negri Primary School, Uganda

Some people, like myself, collect water for their daily use from rivers or lakes. Others get it from taps. I actually think that we can learn a lot just by telling each other what water means to us and how the need for it affects our daily life. This is why I want to start this book by telling you more about myself and what water means to me. Later on, I will definitely be interested in knowing more about you and what water means to you. So, why don't you try to compare my story with yours while reading!

I live in a village called Musembe with my parents and my five brothers. My village is located in a beautiful countryside area with many green hills. It is about 500 kilometres from the city of Nairobi. Our house is built on a hillside on my grandfather's farm. Although it used to be a large farm we only have about two acres left after the original 20 acres were divided amongst my grandfather's ten sons.

Dian Nikolaev Nikolov, Peyo Yavorov School, Bulgaria

In the days of my grandfather, land was large, food was plenty, and water was in its purest form. Nowadays everyone in our village seems to be struggling. Life in the village is quite challenging. At the same time it is interesting and often very eventful.

On an ordinary weekday, I wake up at six o'clock in the morning. Being the only girl in our family, I have to help my mother do house chores before I run to school. The first thing is to ensure that there is enough water for bathing and preparing tea for breakfast.

Yesterday, for instance, I didn't fetch water in the evening, because I got home late after a long day in school. So today I have to run down to the stream in the valley to collect water. Going down the valley is easy. But coming back is a steep three kilometres uphill task.

Early in the morning is the best time to collect water. The water is still cold and very clean. Later the water will become dirty. This is because during the day many people will have dipped their containers into the small pool of water by the spring from where we all draw.

The herd boys will also come and bring their cattle to drink. The sheep are well behaved as they drink from the sides. However, goats can be funny. They seem to want to explore the aquatic plants in the water; and they always have their way because the boys get carried away as they swim in the lower parts of the stream and forget to look after the goats.

Richard Njenga Waitumbi, Kisumu Jnr Academy, Kenya

Nthabi fetching water

I envy those boys, they can spend hours swimming. They sometimes go to the extent of making rafts to row themselves downstream. The only problem is that their cattle and goats roam around making the water very muddy and dirty.

If you come late you must wait for the others to fetch first. The elderly ladies draw first followed by older girls before the younger girls can be given an opportunity.

We use calabashes to draw the water. Oh, I forgot that some of you might never have seen a calabash! I think that many of you don't even have calabashes in your countries. A calabash is a type of fruit, which grows on the ground, just like a pumpkin. When the fruit matures we take out the inside. This leaves us with an empty hard shell, which can be cut into two pieces. When cut, the calabash serves as a type of spoon, which is very suitable for drawing water.

In my village there are some people who don't have calabashes, instead they use small plastic containers or jugs. However, a calabash is often preferred because it doesn't stir up the water. I guess this is due to its shape, it is round underneath and you don't have to dip it so deep in the river when collecting the water.

The elderly ladies usually come to wash their clothes at the stream. Young girls are not allowed to do this, as it is claimed we still have energy to carry enough water to do our washing at home.

After drawing the water, I start walking back home. But this time it is not easy. First of all, I am now carrying 25 litres of water on my head. Mr. Koze, my teacher told me that every one litre of water weighs one kilogram. That means that I am now carrying 25 kilograms on my head; it is actually heavy! But I don't complain because every girl of my age in our village is now used to this task.

Secondly, the return trip is uphill. It is always on this trip that I realise that the distance between my mother's house and the stream is long. I have been walking for 20 minutes now and yet I am not halfway. I will have to hurry because if I don't leave home by 7.00 a.m. I will be late for school.

Oh! I just remembered that today is Friday. Friday is a good day as pupils look forward to the weekend. However, it is on Fridays that each girl has to go to school with at least five litres of water. This water is used to wash the classrooms. You see, our school doesn't have tap water. Neither do we have a well. But don't get alarmed! In fact, life is better now than it was in past years when the floors of our classrooms were not cemented. At that time, we used to carry both water and cow dung for smearing the floors. When smeared, the cow dung prevents dust from building up on the floor of the classroom.

I haven't told you about Sasha yet, have I? Sasha is my best friend and fortunately we are neighbours. I just hope that she will understand my situation and carry the five litres of water for me to take to school. You know, when it rains like it did last night, Sasha finds it really easy. Her father has an iron-roof house and when it rains on the roof, the water runs from the roof into gutters. From the gutters the water pours into a tank, which he has placed on the ground. The only problem is that their tank is so small that it gets full even before it begins to rain heavily!

Our own house is grass thatched. It is therefore difficult to harvest rainwater. My father tried it once but the water was unsuitable for drinking. It was full of soot from the smoke that collects in the grass from the open firewood stove.

Besides, the banana cutting he used for a gutter would tear off and fall down many times. My father became so wet that he eventually gave up. Sasha's father also used to have banana cutting before he bought the metal gutters. The cuttings had served him relatively well since his house was not grass thatched.

Sasha and I have a secret that we have never shared with anyone else. It is not so easy to guess so I will confide in you. We discovered that rainwater is "sweeter" than water collected from the stream down the valley. So now, every time it rains Sasha and I fill up two small containers and keep them in between banana plants.

This way, the banana plants provide shelter from the sun, rain and mud. We can then draw small amounts from these containers every day and carry in small bottles to school for drinking.

The bottles fit easily into our pockets so the other pupils at school don't bother us when they are thirsty. We sure would love to share with them but we cannot because the sweet water is limited.

You see, we only have rain in certain months of the year. This period is called the rainy season. Rain falls between the months of March and May and between November and December. After the rainy season it will be dry for months on end. Our containers in the banana plantation remain cold and clean even during the dry period. The poem below shows how important rain is, as it provides water and therefore life to humans, animals and plants.

WATER

It rained
Rivers, streams and lakes became full to the brim
Tributaries flow all over without much ado
Scientists came and collected samples of
Water to purify it
Man and animals could not hesitate to enjoy drinking
Cool clean water

Oh water you are such a special commodity
No one can live without you
Leaking taps should be tightly closed
No dripping water should be seen
Anywhere in toilets, kitchens and general usage!!
Dirt runs smoothly when there is water
Sewerage systems
Functions well through the help of water

Plants also grow vigorously when nurtured
All this is possible because of you water

Water! You are a real champion.

Student at Matswathaka Primary School, South Africa

This idea also helped us to keep our water cold in the house. We discovered that storing water in clay pots is better than in metal and plastic containers. Metal containers are the worst as they absorb heat from the surrounding and warm up the water inside. I very much wish that my mother would buy us an improved pot for storing water. At least she has promised to buy one when she gets some extra money.

Water is life! An educational booklet on water

21

Water World Chapter 2

I first saw the improved storage pots at the local potter's place when Mr. Koze, our teacher, took our class on a tour to the workshop. What is new is that the potter makes pots with a tap at the bottom. When we asked her what the big idea was, she answered, "it is very easy to waste water if you are drawing it by dipping a container into the main storage pot." This immediately made sense to Sasha and myself.

Surinder Roopra, Kisumu Senior Academy, Kenya

The potter also told us that the local doctor had praised the new design of the pots because it helps to prevent contamination that may occur when dipping dirty containers into the pot. "This type of clay pot simply removes the danger of someone with dirty hands from ever contaminating the drinking water," she said. "Many waterborne diseases can be avoided using these new pots. Of course, it is better if we take care of the source of water", she added.

The lady seemed to have so much knowledge. We all admired her wisdom. She also told us that planting more trees around the stream would help us to preserve the water in the stream. At this, Sasha looked at me and giggled. At that time the teacher thanked the potter and guided us back to school.

Recalling all this makes me think of how I can improve the quality of the water we draw from the stream. I will try the boiling method we recently learnt at school. What was it Mr. Koze was talking about? I think he mentioned that boiling the water kills something called germs. Yes, now I remember! He said that water collected from the stream might contain germs and that another word for germs is microorganisms. He also said that microorganisms cause many diseases that can be transmitted through water.

MICROORGANISMS

Microorganisms are very small living things; you cannot even see them with naked eyes. The only way to see them is through a microscope. They exist everywhere in nature and not all of them cause diseases. In fact, we would not be able to survive without them and most of them are doing very important jobs in nature.

When I return from school tonight I will boil the water I collected from the stream this morning. My mother will definitely be very happy with me once she finds out what I am doing. In due course I am sure that she will buy us the improved pot I have longed for since that trip to the potter!

Activity Box

What does water mean to you? Reflect over what role water play in your own life. Form small discussion groups with your classmates or friends and describe to each other an ordinary day in your lives and how water is involved in it. What are the differences and similarities between your story and Nthabi's? Is there something you can learn from what Nthabi has just been telling you?

Water is life!
An educational booklet on water
23
Water World
Chapter 2

Do you know water?

Chapter 3

Do you know water?

My school is situated two kilometres from our house. It is called Musembe Primary School. The market where we sell most of our farm produce such as milk, poultry and eggs is actually quite near the school. There are a few shops there too.

I am in standard eight or primary 8, if you like. Next year I will go to secondary school. My favourite subject is Science and Nature Study. Our teacher Mr. Koze is a lovely person, though I sometimes think he gives us too much homework, but my mother says it is because he is concerned and wants us to learn as much as possible.

Something I like about Mr. Koze is that he allows us to explore many things on our own. In fact, it was due to him that Sasha and I got the idea of starting a small activity group on the subject of water in our school.

It all started after the trip we made last term to the local potter. That trip really inspired Sasha and me to find out what we can do in order to learn more about water. There seem to be so much more to know!

DO YOU KNOW WATER?

There is no doubt that all of us must have seen water. You probably are familiar with water in oceans, lakes, seas, rivers, and ponds. In some homes or schools water is available from a tap. In other communities it is drawn from wells, or streams.

Pure water is colourless. It does not smell and is tasteless. Without water there can be no life on Earth.

Water is of major importance to all living things; in some organisms, up to 90 per cent of their body weight comes from water. More than 60 per cent of the human body is water, the brain is composed of 70 per cent water, blood is 82 per cent water, and the lungs are nearly 90 per cent water.

Learning about water is a continuous task. When it comes to water no limits exist, there will always be something new to learn!

When we told Mr. Koze about our interest he became very happy and suggested that we start a study group that same day! He talked to the other teachers in our school and together we formed a group of 15 girls and boys of different ages. We meet every Thursday after classes. We discuss different topics that can help us to learn more about water. We also try to participate in local community activities.

Last Thursday a girl from P5 told the group that she once got to follow her father to see a relative in a village situated quite far from ours. She told us that in that village they had fenced the area around the water spring to prevent animals from getting into the spring where the water is most clean. We all got very exited over her story and decided to take immediate action!

Two representatives from our group visited the village elder to discuss the issue; guess what, not only did he like the idea but he even decided that we immediately start the work the following weekend! Many people from our village have contributed with material for the fencing. The only thing missing now is a packet of nails. I am really looking forward to starting the work!

I can't wait to write to my friends about this new project! Ah, that's right! I haven't yet told you about my friends. I have friends all over the world, in Mexico, Uganda, Finland, Bulgaria, India, South Korea and many more countries. I think I will have to start from where it all began, that is, how I got to know them.

Once every two months we try to summarise what we have discussed in our study group. We do that by writing essays and poems as well as drawing paintings, just like the ones you see in this book. These are then exhibited in our school so that people can come and see what children have to say about water.

The exhibitions are mainly for our parents, classmates and other people from the village. Sometimes Mr. Koze helps us to invite people from outside, such as Government representatives and Education Officers.

Opira Raphael, Gulu Secondary School, Uganda

Sometimes, we also invite children from schools in neighbouring villages to come and see the exhibitions. We are also in contact with some schools situated very far from ours. These children cannot come all the way to our school due to the distance, and instead we write letters to each other. Sometimes, when the exhibitions are over, we pack our work in boxes and big envelopes and send to these schools.

Anyway, by now, we have seen many visitors come to our school to see our exhibits. It was during one of these visits that an Education Officer proposed that our school should be part of a pilot project on the use of computers in schools. After only a few weeks, the Government had donated five computers to our school.

To enable the computers to work in this rural village where there is no electricity, the Government gave us solar panels to generate electricity from the sun. Once the sun shines, the panels transform the sunlight into electricity. The electric power is then stored in batteries and used up slowly to operate the computers.

Later on our school was linked up to the Internet through a microwave link to the college in a nearby town. I don't know how the microwave link works, but I can assure you we are now becoming proficient on searching the Internet.

It's through the Internet that we have come to learn more about what life is like in other parts of the world. Our teacher helped us to look for schools in other countries that were also linked up to the Internet. This way, we make friends from all over the world. Now, we exchange e-mails, that is, letters that can be sent over the Internet, with these friends.

Most of the time my friends and I write to each other about water issues. In some schools you can find the same type of activity groups that we have formed here in our school. Thanks to the Internet, we can now share and compare our work easily.

Vulshebstvo Kindergarten, Bulgaria

It is really amazing to see how much my friends know about water and what they do with their knowledge, not to mention how creative many of them are. Look at this nice poem below for example.

WATER

Water is clear and crystaline
Like the stars that appear on my window
It's song is the most beautiful
Gives me peace which has no other.

It's freshness takes our tiredness away
And takes us to the most beautiful spaces
Water is glory to the plants
Which grow flourishing and enchanting us in every corner.

Water, vital liquid you are a treasure
Must be kept by everybody sacred
The earth becomes greener to the summit
water you will be our treasure forever.

Fernando Gutierrez R., Hebreo Sefaradi, Mexico

Lately, something happened to me which made me appreciate the elderly people around us as a very important source of knowledge. I will tell you the story.

Some weeks ago one of my younger brothers fell sick. He had fever and you know that when you have fever you should drink a lot of water. Though I had already collected water in the morning, my mother told me to go down to the stream once again in the afternoon. We had to ensure that my brother would have enough water to drink during the night. I didn't mind walking that extra trip since I wanted my brother to recover as quickly as possible. My only fear was that I would find the water in the stream too dirty since it was already late in the afternoon.

Unfortunately I was right; the water was extremely muddy and dirty! I sat down in despair, wondering what to do. There was no way my brother could drink that water! Suddenly I saw an old lady coming towards me. I had never seen her face before but I soon remembered that Sasha had told me something earlier that day about her mother having a visitor from Sudan.

The lady came up to me. Seeing my disappointed face she asked, "My dear, you look miserable, what is wrong?" I told her about my brother being ill and then pointed at the dirty water in the stream. She looked at me and said, "Don't worry my daughter, I will help you out".

I waited suspiciously - what did she have in mind? As far as I could see she didn't carry any water so I knew she wouldn't give me any pure water to take home to my brother. While putting down the big bag she was carrying, she asked me "Have you ever heard about Moringa?" I had not, so I said "No, who is Moringa?" The lady laughed, "Moringa is a tree, some people call it a miracle tree because it has so many uses. The leaves are very nutritious and it can cure a number of diseases."

She took something out of her pocket and showed me, "These are seeds of a Moringa tree. The seeds have been used traditionally to purify water for many, many years. In Sudan, where I come from, we use it to purify the water we draw from the River Nile and that water can sometimes be five times as dirty as the one here in your stream!" I looked at her curiously while she continued, "You first remove the outer part of the seed, like this, and then you grind the inner part. After grinding you put the white powder into your dirty water. You then stir for about 20 minutes and after that, you do nothing but wait."

She took a small bowl from her bag and told me to fetch some of the dirty water from the stream. We followed the procedure she had explained. After waiting for some 30 minutes something started to happen in the bowl! I could not believe my eyes! All the dirt started to settle down at the bottom of the bowl, leaving much clearer water on top. I was impressed!

Krupali A. Patel, Kisumu Jnr Academy, Kenya

At the same time, it reminded me of what I had learnt in school about the big water treatment plants. I recalled that in the treatment process, vast amounts of chemicals are often used in order to achieve the same type of sedimentation.

The lady told me that scientists are currently carrying out experiments to find out more about Moringa. She said that in some African countries, Moringa powder has been used as a natural alternative to the chemicals used in large-scale treatment plants.

Before she left, she gave me a small bag of Moringa seeds. When I got home I repeated the procedure before my family. Obviously, they were as impressed as I had been.

However, what I didn't tell them was that I kept a few of the seeds for myself. Before I went to bed that night I sneaked out and planted the remaining seeds a few meters from our house. Please don't tell anyone, I want it to be a surprise! Hopefully these trees will grow big and produce a lot of seeds. I can only imagine how happy my parents will be when they realise that we can use our own Moringa seeds to purify our water, every day.

A DROP OF WATER

It lays upon my window...
And I swim in its transparence
It's clarity and purity.

Drop of water
In your long walk, from the sky to the
mountain
and from the mountain to the sea.

Drop of water
How many more do you
have to add,
for so many rivers pass
and after such a harsh ride
my exsistence realize.

David Benguitat, Hebreo Sefaradi, Mexico

My friend Malshini, from Seychelles sent me a sad story about a young girl who went in search of water for her sick mother. She was not as fortunate as I was when my brother was sick.

Water World Chapter 3 Do you know water? An educational booklet on water

31

JUST A DROP OF WATER!!

"Water! Oh, please, just a little drop of water!" Kamala's mother was crying out in her feverish state.

"Be patient, Mother", said Kamala. "It is midnight; you know the water pipe opens only at four a.m."

"But go now, daughter; the queue will be too long then."

At two a.m. leaning on her two sticks which served as crutches, handicapped Kamala went to the water pipe, clutching a clay pot in her hand, and with a brass pot on her head. She was the tenth there already.

By 3.45 a.m., a long queue had started winding up through the slum. At 4.05 a.m., there was no water coming out of the pipe. People started to get worried, and had started praying; this water pipe was the only one leading into the slums. At 4.10, there was still no water. Then, at 4.15, water started to drip out of the tap. A sigh of relief ran through the queue. One by one, the slum dwellers impatiently started filling their pots with the trickle of water.

Suddenly, a fight broke out; thugs were pushing, shouting and shoving to get to the water pipe first. During the struggle, one of the men fell heavily onto the pipe, and broke it – the only pipe in the slums. Kamala was knocked to the ground during the fight, and, in the process, broke her clay pot.

The authorities who knew no other solution closed the pipe, saying "No more water for two days!"

Kamala returned to her sick mother with an empty brass pot and pieces of the clay pot – whatever she could collect. By evening, her mother's fever rose, and she became delirious. The doctor had said "Give her plenty of liquids." What could Kamala do?

She watched helplessly, as her mother breathed her last – more due to lack of water than due to the fever.

There was just not one drop of water to save her, but another handicapped orphan was added to the number.

Malshini Senaratne, Anse Boileau Secondary School, Seychelles

After my experience with Moringa I now listen to the evening stories my grandparents tell us with greater attention. For instance there is a taboo in my village that a special indigenous tree species found in marshland cannot be used for firewood. I guess this taboo was used in order to preserve the tree so as to protect wetlands, that is the damp areas of land around the stream.

It is unfortunate that most of my age mates dismiss these things because they cannot make sense out of them. I think that we have to listen carefully and take the stories our parents and grandparents tell us seriously so that this type of traditional knowledge is not forgotten. For example, have you ever heard of rainmakers? Last night my grandfather told me that in the past, rainmakers used to come to our village in dry seasons. Apparently, they tried to produce rain by using special dances and drums. A friend of mine from Uganda sent me the following poem about rainmakers.

THE RAINMAKERS PROGRESS

I can feel the deepness of his pain
His every tear and fear
Is met with sneers and jeers

Everybody cries out when he leaves his home
But no one weeps when he is gone
For the failure of his drums and charms
Are but gains for the damned

In this valley
Where the mothers are wastefully sullen
And the children's stomachs are obscenely swollen
The dust of the last has yet to come

Over fields once green
Which now crackle with thirst
With wind, with waste, and dust of a thousand fears
Opening up heaps of ash of a thousand years
As springs where once amorous hearts took flight
Are now but sores for the mourners sight

Our hearts and stomachs are empty
Hoping and wailing
Watching and waiting
For the drumming and charming nears an end
But the rituals wont yield immediately
As Rubanga is yet to have pity and weep
Sending his pain churning storm clouds
To sooth his Forlorn heart,
With pitter patter
Of happy feet
In ditches, in gulleys, and valleys
Drenched in life giving water

I can feel the keeness of the rainmakers gain
His every tear and fear,
Is now met with ululation, cheers and cheers
Every pot will now flow with water, water and more water

Alal B Sophie, Mt. St. Mary's School, Uganda

There are so many ways in which one can learn more about water. Reading books, searching the Internet and talking to your grandparents are just a few examples: but, of course, we have different basic conditions when learning.

Almost everybody can talk to his or her grandparents but not everybody can search the Internet. I just wish that school children all over the world could have the same facilities as we have in our school! It certainly makes the world look smaller!

Daniel Sarfati Weitzner, Hebreo Sefaradi, Mexico

Activity box

What can you do to learn more about water? In your class, try to come up with one suggestion each on what can be done in your particular school in order to gain a deeper understanding of the importance of water!

This is me: H₂O!

Chapter 4

This is me: H₂O!

I think it is now time for my friends and I to share with you some of the facts we have learnt about water. Please be attentive. The first question we have to ask ourselves is: what is water?

The essay below comes from a school in Bulgaria and it gives us a number of useful facts about water.

THIS IS ME: H_2O

A solution
An environment for life
A reactive substance
A product of reactions
A thermoregulator
A polar molecule
A source of energy

Water – a word with five letters, everyone is familiar with this chemical formula (H_2O), this substance needed by every form of life.

The distribution of water use in one day by a family of four is:
75% - bathing
20% - cleaning and laundry
5% - drinking and cooking

Water can be polluted by the use of excess detergents and cleaning materials.

Suggested alternatives for some cleaning materials:

Preparation for:	Cleaning material:	Alternative
Tiles	Poisonous chemicals with corrosive effects	A solution of baking soda
Windows	Poisonous chemicals with corrosive effects	Hot water and vinegar in a 11 : 1 proportion
Stove, sink, counters	Strong poisonous bases, which can cause burns	Clean with baking soda

Students at Dobrudja Technical School, Bulgaria

A glass of water consists of many, very small parts which you cannot see with your own eyes. These parts are called molecules. Each molecule of water contains two parts of hydrogen and one part of oxygen. One molecule of water is very, very tiny. It is much smaller than the microorganisms I mentioned earlier. In a glass of water, you will find billions of water molecules! The chemical symbol for hydrogen is H and that for oxygen is O. Now, you can easily understand why the chemical formula for water is H_2O.

Our teacher Mr. Koze told us that H_2O can exist in three physical states: ice, (solid state), water (liquid state), and as water vapour (gaseous state). He also told us that the amount of water in the world always remains the same and that the water is said to go through a cycle, called the water cycle.

THE WATER CYCLE

When the sun shines on Earth the heat causes water from the seas and the lakes to evaporate. The water vapour then rises up into the sky. As it goes up it meets cold air and forms clouds. Clouds consist of very tiny drops of water. Once the cloud has become dense, the drops will become big and will fall on the ground as rain. Rainwater is partly absorbed by the soil and the vegetation and partly runs off into rivers, streams and lakes and eventually a great part of it will end up where it actually came from, that is, in the sea. This way, water is said to go through the water cycle.

Water Cycle

Now you know in what forms water exist. How about the water you use every day, where do you get it from? Sources of water can be divided into three main groups. These three groups are surface water, groundwater and seawater. I will try to explain each of the three groups separately. The water we can use for drinking is called freshwater. Surface water and groundwater are the only two sources of freshwater on Earth.

SURFACE WATER

Most of our drinking water comes from surface water. Sources of surface water include dams, lakes, rivers and ponds. The Great Lakes basin situated in Canada and the United States is one of the Earth's largest freshwater systems. Lake Baikal in Russia is another large source of surface water. Also the Amazon River in Brazil in South America carries enormous amounts of water. It actually flows through the entire northern half of the continent!

In school, Mr. Koze once showed us a picture of the Amazon River. It looked so beautiful with a lot of big, leafy trees hanging down in the water. Unfortunately, Brazil is situated very far from Kenya so I cannot go there and see it myself. Instead, we have to find other ways of sharing the beauty of water. I think that our friend Paul really has succeeded with that in his nice poem below.

WATER

Water, Water so beautifully blue
It flows from end to end
It shines so bright under the sun
And makes you feel so warm inside
We take it day by day
And still it doesn't run out
Oh what a blessing God has given us
That we may cherish it!

Paul Ogbuigwe, Stanborough School, United Kingdom

Here in Africa our biggest lake is Lake Victoria, which is actually the second largest freshwater body in the whole world. Part of Lake Victoria is situated in Kenya but most of it is shared between our neighbouring countries, Uganda and Tanzania.

In dry parts of the world, that is, the arid and semi-arid areas, there is practically no surface water. The seasonal rivers are dry most of the time. In fact, if you were told that they are rivers you wouldn't believe it. It is only when it rains heavily in the upper part of the stream that they get filled with water. However, in many areas the streams dry up quickly after the rain. Surface water cannot be considered a reliable water source in such places. For people living in these areas, getting enough water for their daily use can be rather tough.

© kello Deogracious Omuk, Gulu High School, Uganda

I once had a personal experience of how hard life must be when there is no reliable water source. This was when our stream dried up completely during a drought. It was very sad because the whole village depended on that stream for water.

My grandfather told me that long ago the stream never used to dry up. There was always enough water for people and animals. He also told me that nobody was ever allowed to cultivate the land near the stream and its wetlands. When it rains, a lot of water is conserved in the wetland. This stored water will later on slowly pour into the nearby lakes and rivers. Unfortunately, people now drain the wetlands for agriculture. My grandfather suspects this might be one reason why our only source of freshwater is drying up.

My grandfather's suspicion actually agrees with what Mr. Koze told us in school the other day. He said that the number of people had increased a lot in the area around the stream in the last two decades; and, of course, with a higher number of people the demand for water and other natural resources increases as well.

This is a typical problem in many African countries today. Luckily, in our village we have now come to understand how important it is to conserve the areas around rivers. We have to stop depleting the vegetation around our small stream if we want to continue having water!

Ruth Wanjiru, Makini School, Kenya

When it rains, surface water systems such as rivers and lakes receive a lot of water in the form of run-off. If the area where the rain reaches the Earth contains a lot of pollutants, these pollutants will follow the run-off and sooner or later the whole water sources will be polluted. This is one reason why so many surface water sources today are under threat of pollution.

GROUNDWATER

The first time I heard about groundwater was the time when our stream dried up. Our village was hit by severe drought and it had not rained for over eight months. When the situation started to become serious, the village elder sent for a Government Official to come and help us. It was this Government Official who told us that we could get water from underneath the ground.

To be honest, I found that statement rather strange so the next day I asked our teacher if there really is water under the earth. He said, "The answer is yes, Nthabi. There is water in the ground." Sasha and I giggled when we heard this because it confirmed what the Government Official had told our village elder. However, we still did not understand how water collects underground. Is it in rivers, or is there an underground sea?

Noticing our blank stares Mr. Koze explained, "Rainwater and water from melting ice slowly penetrates into the ground. The water moves very, very slowly through tiny pores or spaces in the soil. Porous rocks can also allow water to run through them."

Mr. Koze added that, "Some of the groundwater ends up in aquifers under ground and can be obtained by drilling boreholes or digging wells. The depth at which groundwater can be found varies a lot, some boreholes and wells can be shallow like 3 meters and others very deep like 300 meters."

When we walked home from school that day we found that the village elder had already called for a number of strong men to start digging up for water. But the Government Official who fortunately was still around said, "No, you must first get a water expert to survey your village for groundwater. He will help you to locate the best place to dig. After that, the village can apply for a license to sink a well."

He explained that groundwater needs to be well managed. If not, we could end up drying up streams and rivers in other villages. In addition he said that it is important to take samples of the water for laboratory analysis to find out if the water is fit for drinking.

"Groundwater travels long distances. It is easy for the water to be polluted at some point far away from here. Fertilisers and herbicides used on commercial farms such as flower farms, as well as chemicals discharged from industries, can find their way into the soil and contaminate the groundwater", the Government Official added.

Groundwater is the only source of freshwater for lots of people in many parts of the world.

SEAWATER

Seawater is another main source of water. It actually makes up about 97% of all the water on Earth. Everyone who has seen a map of our world knows that the seas and oceans contain a lot of water. If you take a close look you will find that there is more water than there is land. Around two-thirds of the surface of the Earth is covered with water!

Now, you may ask yourself: If two-thirds of the Earth is covered with water, how come so many people around the world don't have enough for their basic need? Don't worry, you are not alone in this. I used to ask myself the same question but found the answer a few months ago when I had the chance to go to Mombasa with one of my elder brothers. Mombasa is a large town, situated on the coast of the Indian Ocean in the eastern part of Kenya.

The bus trip to get there was long and the weather extremely hot. When we finally arrived, my brother took me down to the sea so that we could wash ourselves. Reaching the seaside I could not believe my eyes - I had never seen so much water in my whole life! It seemed as if the sea didn't have an end. It was so beautiful! Not to mention the sounds of the waves reaching the shores. I was amazed.

When I went down to the water to wash my face, I noticed something peculiar. The water was salty! And it was definitely not suitable for drinking. My brother just laughed at me and told me that all seas and oceans are composed of salty water.

When I got back to school I just had to ask Mr. Koze where all the salt came from. He answered, "When rain falls on rocks and soil, salt is released and dissolves in the water. Since you are now familiar with the water cycle you know that the water that comes in the form of rain sooner or later ends up in the sea. When the water evaporates the salt stays behind and the concentration of the salt in the water increases. This process has been going on for millions and millions of years. Now, imagine the accumulated amounts of salt that has been transported from the land into the sea during all these years!"

Later I read that researchers all over the world are now trying to find new ways to remove salt from the seawater in order to make it drinkable. This is however not the only problem with seawater. Pollution is another big issue. Many big cities are situated in coastal areas and unfortunately much of the waste generated on land ends up in the sea.

Now you have learnt more about the three main sources of water: but, of course, there are various ways of collecting water, like rainwater harvesting.

Jenny Motola Stern, Hebreo Sefaradi, Mexico

CRYSTAL CLEAR RAINBOW,

The singing of the birds and the calmness of the mountain,
Mix together with sounds of water
Sweet voice, crystaline liquid of life
The landscape of a beautiful waterfall
Iluminated with solar rays,
Form a beautiful rainbow

How wonderful life is with such a delight!
Nature as a painting
Makes you feel how life can be real
Cold water refreshes my body,
Which feels it with tenderness,
Precious liquid you are vital to life

Diego Guiterrez, Hebreo Sefaradi, Mexico

If you want to drink water just as crystal clear as the rainbow, you should start harvesting rainwater, like Sasha's father is doing. The rain actually represents one of the purest forms of water that you can find on Earth. I guess this is because it has not yet come in contact with anything dirty; but, of course, if you stay in a big city this will not be the case.

The air in many towns and in areas close to big factories can be full of poisonous gases. When it rains, these gases dissolve in the water and reach the ground together with the rain. When the rainwater gets polluted like this it cannot be used for drinking. In rural areas this problem is not as serious as in big cities though airborne pollutants can travel quite long distances in the air. Actually, many people in rural areas all over the world harvest rainwater and use it for drinking.

One of my friends from India sent me an e-mail saying that in his country rainwater harvesting has been incorporated into the new building rules. Each new building must have gutters and a storage tank for the rainwater.

There are many ways in which rainwater can be harvested. Last year we went on a field trip to one of the dry areas of our country where rivers are only seasonal. When it is not raining the communities have to dig deep in the riverbeds to get some water. However, I must confess that my countrymen and women can be very innovative!

G. Reinu Shyle, India

By the end of the first day of our field trip we passed by a large community where the people had found a very clever solution to the problem of water scarcity. The method was simple and made it possible to provide water to thousands of people and some for irrigating crops.

The method used involved scooping off the soil from a large area to create something like a pan. The rainwater then collects into the earth pan and is stored there even after the rain stops. In this way the community can have water supply during the dry months. Some of the people who took the water from this pan also used a simple filtration process to make the water cleaner.

These people knew, just like you and me, that when the water is meant for drinking, it has to be very clean. But water can be used in many other ways than just for drinking.

Incidentally, Uses of Water was the topic of discussion in our study group last week. Below, Sasha and I have tried to summarise the main points we talked about last Thursday.

Water to support life

Without water, there can never be life on Earth. Animals, birds, fishes, insects and plants all need water to live. The human body is about 65 per cent water. Some plants, such as aquatic plants that live in water, can even contain more than 90 per cent of water.

Water for domestic use

We use water quite a lot in our homes. When we wake up in the morning the first thing most of us do is to brush out teeth, wash our face and sometimes even take a bath. During the day we have to eat and water is an important ingredient in almost everything we cook. After eating, we clean our utensils and for that, we must use water. Also the clothes we wear need to be washed every now and then - a process that consumes a lot of water.

Water for sewage and waste disposal

Do you know what happens once you flush a toilet? Apart from cleaning the toilet the water actually plays a very important role in providing a medium through which human waste is carried away from homes. The water then eventually reaches a sewage treatment plant where the waste is removed and the water treated before it is discharged in nature again.

Water for agriculture

Agriculture is the major consumer of freshwater in our world. Especially in dry areas huge amounts of water is used for agricultural purposes. All crops and vegetables that we eat everyday need water in order to grow. Crops and vegetables often need more water than they can get from the natural rains. In such cases the farmers have to provide them with additional water - they have to irrigate their cultivated land.

Water in industry

Almost all industries use water at some stage in their production cycle. Some industries use water for cooling their machines. When water is made to pass outside the hot containers, heat gets transferred into the water, which itself becomes heated. Water can take large amounts of heat. In addition almost all industries use water for cleaning. Some industries also use water as an essential ingredient in their products, such as in sodas and beers or in the chemical industry to dissolve chemicals.

Water to generate power

Water can be made to pass through turbines at a high speed. As the turbines turn they cause a large generator to produce electricity. Many countries have built dams for this purpose. The electricity obtained from such a system is called hydroelectric power.

Water to transport goods and people

Many goods that have to move from one continent to another are transported over water in ships. The movement of cars from Japan to Africa, radios from Germany to Latin America, oil from Kuwait to Europe are a few examples. It is often cheaper to transport heavy and bulky goods over water than by air or by road. In some countries, rivers and canals are also used for transporting both goods and passengers.

Water for safety

Have you ever seen a house on fire? What did people do to stop it? Since water is an important fire extinguisher they probably called for water and poured it over the fire in order to put it off. In some countries forest fires are common in dry periods of the year and during droughts. When a forest fire breaks out the foresters always pray for rain because rain can effectively put out large forest fires, which could not be put out in any other way.

Water for fun

Recreation is another important use of water that we often take for granted. Many people enjoy swimming, whether it is in a river, in the sea or in a swimming pool. It is lots of fun to go swimming, surfing, water skiing and sport fishing. You could also have fun rowing a boat, or a canoe. In the entertainment industry, splashes and water slides are becoming a main attraction for children in some large towns.

Vandana Pali, Arya Vedic Secondary School, Kenya

Sometimes, it seems as if some people have a tendency of taking water for granted. I think that everybody should reflect over issues such as where water originates from and what we actually use it for. It is only then that we will be able to fully appreciate its importance in life!

Activity box

1. Identify the main freshwater sources in your country. Where does the water that you use at school and at home come from?

2. Make a list of how water is used in your school and in your home. Try to find out for what purpose most of the water is used.

3. From what you have learnt and what you already knew, create a newsletter on water together in your class. Make sure that you circulate it in all classes in your school. This can be done on a regular basis, every week a new water-related topic can be treated.

Taking care of water

Chapter 5

Taking care of water

Water does not belong either to one country, to a group of people or to a single person. I think that water can only belong to nature. To use it, we must "borrow" water from nature.

In the same way, when I feel cold, I can borrow a sweater from Sasha. Since the sweater is not my own I have to be very careful with it and make sure that I return it the way it was. I know that Sasha would be very disappointed if I returned it dirty or torn; and of course, she would never lend it to me again no matter how cold I feel! Liang from China definitely understands what it means to borrow something from nature. Please read her story about Miss Water.

A STORY OF MISS WATER

Teacher: "Good afternoon children! Welcome to our programme. Today, we are going to have an interview with Miss Water, a woman who had a pathetic situation. Miss Water, please tell us about your story."

Miss Water: "All right! Many years ago, I was a pretty girl. I had beautiful looks, my eyes shone like the stars in the sky. My hair was long and meek like the streams. I used to be really neat.

I had many friends! Miss Fish, Mr. Shrimp and Mr. Man were my best friends. We used to play and sing together. We had a very good time!

Mr. Man had the habit of borrowing things from me because I was rich. At first I was glad to help him. But later I found out that he never returned what he had borrowed. But he kept on borrowing things from me. Day after day he became more and more demanding. He even took my things without permission! Mr. Man was so strong that I couldn't stop him from doing that. Thus from there on, I became poorer and poorer. My hair became dry because I lacked the oil to apply to make it soft and meek like the streams. My body became extremely dirty. As a result Miss Fish and Mr. Shrimp suffered as they too depended on me. No one liked me anymore.

Teacher: "Poor thing! How could Mr. Man do that? My dear class, how do you feel after hearing this story?

Xia: "In my opinion, everything should have a limit. Mr. Man should discipline himself! Unless we discipline ourselves we will find that Miss Water will not be our friend. She will simply dry up on us!!"

Liang Jianzin, China

As Liang says, we have to be careful with the water we borrow and return it in the same state, as it was when we first got it. We humans also have to stop being so selfish and understand that we are not the only ones that need water to survive. Try to think of how many animal species you know that live in water. I know at least 20 so I guess the real number must be countless! Fish, shrimps, sharks, octopuses, snails, starfish, dolphins and whales are just a few examples.

Some people actually seem to think that the seas, lakes and streams are just huge dustbins. You can never imagine the enormous amount of garbage that is disposed into water every year. Sewage from cities, poisonous chemicals from factories, expired drugs and other waste products are actually dumped in water on a daily basis.

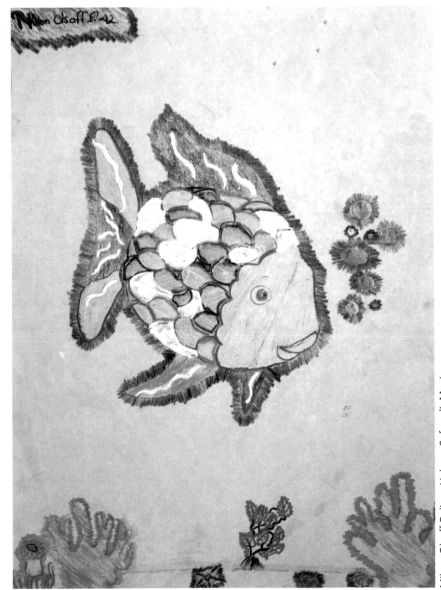

Milton Olsoff Policar, Hebreo Sefaradi, Mexico

Unfortunately, many of the water species are today threatened and some are even disappearing because of all the garbage that we throw into their homes. Imagine if your neighbour came to your house every day and emptied his or her dustbin in your bedroom. It would affect you, wouldn't it? And finally you would have to move.

Have you ever heard of coral reefs? I have never seen one myself but I have heard that coral reefs are really beautiful and are just like the rainforests of the sea. The coral reefs serve as home for enormous numbers of sea species. It is terrible that today more than half of the coral reefs in the world are dying because of sea pollution caused by humans. When the coral reefs are dying the species that live there will lose their homes and eventually they will die too.

We have to respect all species that need water to live and not only think about ourselves. Clearly, we have to take care of the water nature is providing us with, just like Boniface from Kenya writes in the following essay.

TAKING CARE OF WATER

Water is a compound made up of two elements; oxygen and hydrogen. Presence of water in the environment is important to living things to enhance and sustain life process. Also, water has been largely used in man-made machines for efficient functioning. Human beings use water for domestic purposes and also for drinking.

Though water is regarded as essential to human life, some factors have led to pollution of water. Such factors include chemicals used in agriculture that normally get washed away by rain to the rivers. Rainwater also carries harmful bacteria into rivers and ponds. Untreated industrial wastes directly discharged into rivers as well as poisonous fumes from large industries also pollute rainwater. Some fumes released into the atmosphere cause acid rain.

Factors that cause shortage of water include desertification and destruction of water catchment zones. When trees are cut down without re-planting the result is a shortage of water vapour in the atmosphere from which rain droplets can be formed.

The increase in the level of greenhouse gases has caused much heating on land thus causing seasonal rivers to dry up. Many places also have inadequate water storage facilities, which lead to wastage of a lot of water.

To prevent shortage and pollution of water, we need to take action. Firstly, land near rivers should not be cultivated. This will ensure that water sources are not clogged with soils. Also the chemicals used to grow crops on such land should be reduced.

Domestic chores such as washing clothes should be carried out away from water sources. Industries must be made to treat their wastes before releasing into rivers. This also can be improved further by setting special places aside where wastes can be deposited instead of directly into the river.

Factories that release fumes that may cause acidic rain must stop releasing these fumes because many people depend on rainwater for drinking, bathing and washing. People should also be educated to avoid using asbestos sheets for roofing their houses if they use rainwater for domestic purposes because asbestos sheets release poisonous substances when rainwater falls on them.

Boniface Kedogo, Chavalaki High School, Kenya

Another damaging product, which every year runs into our water in large amounts, is oil. The oil can originate from street run-off, from industrial effluents or from accidents involving big tankers transporting oil on water. The other day, I received an e-mail from Emil, a Swedish friend of mine. His story taught me a lot about what can happen to the surrounding environment when oil is released in water.

Sweden is a beautiful country situated in the northern part of Europe. The country borders the Baltic Sea to the east. Many types of goods are transported on ships on the Baltic Sea and oil is one of them.

My friend Emil lives in the south eastern part of Sweden in an area which is known for its nice beaches. Summer is Emil's favourite season. This is not just because he is free from school and can spend all day playing with his friends but because it is the time when many people from all parts of Sweden come to his home area to spend their holidays swimming and relaxing by the sea. Some of Emil's best friends stay in cities far away and they only meet during summer holidays. This year, by the time summer approached Emil was waiting eagerly for his friends to come.

Nicole Smith, Weston Coyney Sec. School, United Kingdom

Unfortunately, Emil wrote in the e-mail he sent me, this summer didn't turn out to be as it had been in the preceding years. Just when the holiday was about to start, Emil read in the newspapers that a foreign tanker transporting oil on the Baltic Sea had grounded just outside the Danish coast, quite close to the place in Sweden where he lives. Apparently the ship was not built safely enough and soon oil started to leak out from it.

In school Emil had learnt about oil spills and environmental damage related to it. So he immediately understood that the news was very bad. It was clear that he was not going to see so many of his friends this summer! As he had suspected, some of the oil that had leaked out from the ship eventually reached the Swedish coast. It had terrible consequences as Emil writes in the letter, "Our beaches used to be so beautiful. Now, some of them are more or less covered with thick black oil. There is no way we will see tourists on these beaches this year!"

However, it wasn't the fact of not seeing his friends that bothered him the most. He says in the letter, "What makes me really sad is to see all the animals, especially the birds and fishes that have been stuck in the oil. Many of them died." He also wrote that many people from his town volunteered to help in the cleaning process.

CONTAMINACIÓN DEL AGUA

Armando Valdez Mandujano, Angel Matute Vidal, Mexico

Emil himself assisted a local biologist to help birds that had survived but had got oil in their feathers. Some of these birds recovered quite quickly whereas others would never be able to swim or fly again. Thanks to the effort put in by the people from Emil's town the cleaning process was speeded up considerably.

Actually, Emil is not the only one of my friends who writes to me about problems with oil spills in water. Jelena from Croatia, for example, underlines the dangers related to oil spilled in water in the essay below. It is a worldwide problem that all countries have to deal with together. Just look at the accident Emil was telling us about; the tanker was from a foreign country, it grounded on Danish water but the damage to the environment was in Sweden. To me this is not fair! It is clear that we need enforcement of the international safety laws so that such kind of catastrophes can be avoided.

WATER

Water is our most precious thing on Earth. We use it for drinking, washing, cleaning. We use it in the house, school, everywhere, we even have it inside our bodies. By reading this someone could think that water is the thing every man, woman and child save and take a good care of. But instead of saving, we pollute water. That's why we have it less every day. Sea is also water. Soda cans, papers, and food laying on the beach or swimming in the sea is nothing new.

The biggest polluting of water we do by throwing oil in seas and rivers. It takes years to clean that place, but even then it won't be the same. By polluting the water, we don't pollute just a thing we use every day, but also ourselves and fish who live there. Many people love eating fish, but if we keep polluting, there won't be any fish left. There won't be clean water. While we brush our teeth, or take a bath we leave water running. It is a way of spending too much water.

How can we save water and not pollute it? We have to throw paper, cans, and other garbage in suitable places, but also stop throwing oil in seas, and use water only for our needs, which means we don't have to leave the tap open while brushing our teeth. We have to save water because it is the most important to us. As an Eco-School, we use water the way we need it and don't use it too much. We know that water is very important for our lifes. We should do everything we can to save water and our environment.

Jelena Simic, Vladimir Gortan Primary School, Croatia

Like the Baltic Sea, many water bodies are shared between different countries or on a local level between different villages. For example, people from three different nations depend on Lake Victoria as a source of drinking water. The waste discharged from a Tanzanian town will sooner or later affect the people in Uganda and vice versa.

During last term in school, we learned about River Nile. Mr. Koze told us that River Nile is one of the longest rivers in the world. It flows from Lake Victoria all the way up to the Mediterranean Sea. On the way, it supplies millions of people with freshwater. For instance, many people in the desert part of Egypt depend on it for their daily water needs. These people rely on upstream countries like Uganda and Sudan not to pollute the water before it reaches Egypt. You can now understand why cooperation and respect for other people's needs is crucial when it comes to water. Everybody has the right to have access to clean water since it is a source of life, just like my friend Nelicia writes in her poem below.

SOURCE OF LIFE

More precious than gold or silver

More valuable than money or diamonds

So rare and so little in amount

Two billion people are dying for it

Without a drop to drink

A few days ago there was enough for us all

Where has it all gone?

As if it just vanished into thin air

Did the creator reclaim it all

Who knows?

Now we know that every drop counts

When it is too late

Nelcia Kilindo, Anse Boileau Secondary School, Seychelles

Another important reason why cooperation is required is that freshwater is unevenly distributed in our world. Some areas have a lot of water, others have too little. Too little water or water shortage can sometimes be described as water stress.

WATER STRESS

Water stress occurs when the demand for water threatens to exceed the available water supply. If there is less than 1,000 cubic metres of water per person per year, a country is considered to suffer from water scarcity. If a country has between 1,000 cubic metres and 1,700 cubic metres per person per year it is considered to suffer from water stress. Water stress is an increasing problem in many countries. The problem is most acute in Africa and in West Asia.

Okumu Peter, Gulu High School, Uganda

Today, the population in the world is increasing rapidly. Just like in my village. More people mean a greater need for water. First of all, more people mean that more water will be needed for drinking, washing and cooking. Secondly, with more people around we will need to grow more food. At least in my village where the climate is quite dry we have to irrigate the land that we cultivate. It is now easy to understand that the result of the increase of people in our village as well as in the rest of the world is a considerable increase in the consumption of water.

More people also mean more waste such as human sewage. In my village like in most rural areas in developing countries, we rely on nature alone for treating our sewage. Wetlands, for example, serve as excellent natural treatment systems by filtrating and absorbing much of the nutrients in the sewage.

However, when there is too much sewage we need to construct treatment plants that can help to treat the sewage before it is discharged into nature. In cities, constructed treatment plants are common. They can be of different sizes and they can use different methods for treating the sewage.

Unfortunately, there are not enough wastewater treatment plants in many developing countries. Most of the sewage ends up being discharged untreated. As I mentioned, natural systems such as wetlands can treat some of it but just as a constructed treatment plant has a certain capacity, natural systems also do. There is a limit to how much sewage nature can treat. I agree with Emmanuel who sent me the poem below; why do we have to dump our wastes in water?

WATER! WATER! WATER!

Water the mother and the father of life
The answer to the most essential thing for life is water
Plants animals and man need water

Water! Water! Water!
The tropical people who have it available to them don't conserve it
The desert people are dying for it
I cry to the industrialist
Why dump your waste in water to pollute it
Not knowing you are destroying the life of a billion people

Water! Water! Water!
Water is so natural
Water is so cool and refreshing
No human being can neither manufacture nor make it

Water! Water! Water!
I cry to the warriors
Why test your missile in water
Not thinking of a billion lives you are destroying by water pollution

Water! Water! Water!
Agriculturalist
Plant more trees to maintain the water cycle
Protect and conserve the wetlands
You will have protected the life of a billion people

Emmanual Ojara, Gulu Secondary School, Uganda

Yogesh M. Patel, Kisumu Jnr Academy, Kenya

Human sewage as well as fertilisers used for agricultural purposes contain a lot of nutrients, mainly nitrogen and phosphorus compounds. When the nutrients reach the water systems they are consumed by the vegetation in and around the water systems and cause overgrowth. This process is called eutrophication.

EUTROPHICATION

When too many nutrients, often in form of sewage or fertilisers, reach a water body such as a lake, they cause overgrowth of both the plants around the lake and the algae inside it. Algae are small plant organisms that live in water. The algae will cloud the water and block the sunlight from reaching the bottom of the lake. This is disastrous since many underwater plants are dependent on sunlight in order to grow. These plants in their turn provide food and shelter for many water species including some fish and crabs. When the plants die these species lose their habitat, which eventually will lead to their death as well.

Secondly, the sewage and fertilisers themselves as well as the excess dead plants and algae material, contain a lot of organic material. When this material sinks to the bottom and is degraded, a lot of oxygen is consumed. Just like you and me, fish and other organisms living in water need oxygen to survive. When there is not enough oxygen, the fishes as well as some important plant species will die. Eventually the result of eutrophication is a dead lake!

Sewage and other types of waste in our environment also create serious health risks for us humans. Disease-causing bacteria and other microorganisms originating from sewage can easily contaminate our water. Here in Kenya, contaminated water is a big problem.

Do you recall when my younger brother was sick and I had to make an extra tour to the stream? Though he had sufficient amounts of water to drink that night, he didn't feel better the following morning. In fact, his fever had risen and my mother and I decided to take him to the local medical doctor.

While there, the doctor examined my brother for quite a long time. It was after taking a blood test that the doctor found out what was wrong with him. She said that he suffered from something called typhoid fever. I had never heard about it before but looking at my mother's face I understood that it was quite serious.

I anxiously asked the doctor what it meant and she answered, "Typhoid fever is a relatively common disease in many developing countries. It is often transmitted through polluted water in the same way as other serious diseases such as cholera and dysentery. If it is not treated, it can eventually lead to death."

The doctor must have seen the fear in my eyes because she gently held my hand and added, "but don't worry my friend, I am going to give your brother some medicine that will fight the bacteria in his body. I promise you that he will be all right in a couple of days."

As the doctor gave us the medicine she said, "It is clear that we have less water in our stream but it also seems as if the quality of the water has become worse. Lately I have noticed a considerable increase in cases of waterborne diseases in our village. Waterborne diseases are diseases that are spread through water. It is very important that we stop polluting the water in order to prevent the spreading of these types of diseases."

Before we left she gave me a list of preventive measures to be taken for this purpose. The list included measures such as boiling water before drinking and washing hands thoroughly and frequently, especially before handling food. Another important measure was to prevent sewage from both humans and animals from entering the water sources. The sewage has to be disposed of in safe places far from the stream. If not, the sewage can easily be carried to the river with the rainwater.

I immediately thought that waterborne diseases and prevention of their spread would be an excellent topic for the next meeting with our activity group in school!

Water shortages as well as water pollution are serious threats facing our world's population today. But too much water can be problematic, too! In some areas in the world floods are frequent and they cause enormous damage. Sometimes, even whole cities can suffer serious damage as a result of heavy rains that never seem to end. However, I recently came to know that rain alone does not have to be the only cause of floods.

Falguni Popat, Loreto Conv. Msongari, Kenya

Cheng Lut Ming, Hong Kong

I used to be very confused when reading in the newspaper about floods in parts of Kenya that are normally very dry. I must confess that I found it so strange and difficult to imagine. Luckily I now know better, thanks to Anisur, a friend of mine from Bangladesh who knows very much about floods. Bangladesh is a country in South Asia, next to India.

In Bangladesh they have a lot of experience with floods. Anisur explained to me in an e-mail that when we humans change the surface of the Earth it can affect how often and in what areas floods occur. Do you remember what I told you about wetlands earlier? When it rains, wetlands act like a sponge and stores the extra water. Also soil by itself can effectively store water. You can now easily understand that when we drain wetlands for agriculture or cover large areas of land in cities with concrete to build houses, this storage space disappears and the extra water has nowhere to go. The result is that the water instead floods other areas where it can cause a lot of harm.

Disasters related to floods, droughts and water pollution affect millions of people today. Normally, these are problems that cannot be solved by one country, one government or one village on its own. We all have to cooperate and contribute in order to control these threats. Together, we can take care of water!

ACTIVITY BOX: What is happening to water in your country? Do you have any problems with too much, too little or too polluted water? What can you do to change some of your habits in order to save water? Discuss together in the class and come up with a list of these changes. Put the list somewhere in your school where it can be visible to all pupils.

Water World
is in your hands!

Water World is in your hands!

It seems as if our journey is coming to an end. I hope that you have learnt one or two things on the way; but most of all, my wish is that you have discovered the world of water! My friends and I have tried to guide you in our Water World and now it is time for you to create your own.

You see, everybody has his or her own relationship with water. What water means to me in my life or what it means to my friend Emil in his life is most likely quite different from what it means to you in your life. However, we should never stop discussing these differences. Sharing and comparing knowledge is crucial when one wants to learn more about water!

But knowing about water is not enough. What is more important is how to apply the things we have learnt. I mean, the water in the stream in my village does not get purer just because I know it is dirty! After learning we have to take action and use our knowledge in order to change and improve the situation.

Most water sources in our world today are shared between many people and sometimes between several countries. We therefore have to cooperate and respect each other's needs! The water I pollute today might be crucial for somebody else tomorrow. When it comes to water it is not good to be selfish!

Through my friends I have learnt that no matter where I stay, in Kenya or in Sweden, if I am a human, a shrimp, a cat or a tree, I will always need water. We all have to respect and protect the water in our world!

Hey! I am getting late for school. I will quickly take a bath, brush my teeth, take a cup of tea and run to school. Sasha my friend, remember to carry some water for me, for today is Friday!

Nthabi running to school

Water World
Chapter 6

69

Water World is in your hands!
An educationa booklet on water

Glossary

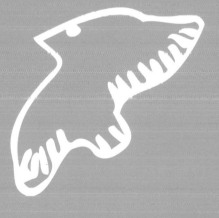

Chapter 7

'70 '73

Glossary

The purpose of this glossary is to enable the reader to fully understand the text in this book. It is not comprehensive but specific to the book.

Algae
Small "plant-like" organisms that are phototrophic, i.e. they can obtain energy from sunlight.

Aquifer
An underground layer of earth, gravel or porous rocks where water can be trapped.

Bacteria
Microscopic organisms that exist everywhere in nature.

Borehole
A narrow well obtained through drilling.

Contamination
Pollution of land, water or air. Contamination can be described as the presence of pollutants, such as chemical substances, sewage and bacteria, that are hazardous to the environment and human health.

Evaporation
The movement of water from the Earth to the atmosphere as vapour.

Fertiliser
A chemical or biological substance that renders soils more fertile and increases its capacity to support plant growth.

Filtration
A process where undissolved particles are mechanically separated from a liquid.

Habitat
The place where an organism lives.

Herbicide
A chemical substance that is used to inhibit the growth of plants, often used to control weeds.

Internet
A system of networks that connects computers all around the world.

Molecule
The smallest unit of a substance that retain the chemical and physical properties of that substance.

Nutrients
Substances that promote growth.

Organic material
Decomposed remains of animals and plants in the soil. Organic material serves as food sources for microorganisms.

Pollutants
Refers to polluting substances such as soil particles, human and animal droppings or wastes, industrial wastes, chemicals, bacteria, microorganisms in general and dead insects and animals in water.

Porous rocks
Rocks with small spaces or holes that allow liquid to pass through them.

Run-off
Water that is not absorbed by the soil or vegetation and instead and runs along the surface of the Earth into rivers, lakes and other lower areas such as for example agricultural land.

Sedimentation
Removal of solid particles in liquid. The particles settle to the bottom of a container or a natural system through gravity.

Sewage
Liquid domestic or industrial waste that can contain solid material and that is carried away in drains or sewers.

Turbine
Can be described as a bladed rotor. When water passes through the turbine, energy from the movement of the water is converted into mechanical power.

Waterborne diseases
Diseases that can be spread through water. Some examples of waterborne diseases are typhoid fever, cholera and dysentery.

Well
A deep hole into the earth, created in order to obtain water.

Wetland
Swampy area of land with vegetation that can grow easily in wet environments.

SOURCES

Environmental Glossary - Dooley and Kirkpatrick - Pira International, 1993
Dictionary of Environment and Sustainable Development - Gilpin - Wiley, 1997
Dictionary of Environmental Science and Technology - Porteous - Wiley, 2000

Questions
and answers

Chapter 8

Questions and answers

Maybe some of you were already aware of the facts you have come across in this book. However, knowledge has no limits; there will always be something new to learn! There are a lot of resources for those of you who want to read more about water and environmental issues.

For example, have you ever heard about reference books such as the Global Environment Outlook, the Africa Environment Outlook and Water for People, Water for life - the United Nations World Water Development Report? It was actually Mr. Koze who introduced these books to our activity group. The books have proved to be very useful for our discussions!

If you don't have access to these books you can always search the UNEP homepage; *www.unep.org*. If you then click on "information for young persons" you will find a number of useful facts, games and links related to water and other environmental issues. My favourites are the exciting Children and Youth UNEP publications called Pachamama and Tunza!

After reading this book I am sure that you will have come up with many questions that you want to have answered. The sources I mentioned above will help you in your research. Children from all over the world have already sent me a number of questions and my teacher Mr. Koze has been kind enough to help me in answering some of them below.

1. WHAT IS WATER SCARCITY?
Water scarcity occurs when the amount of water withdrawn from lakes, rivers or groundwater is so great that water supplies are no longer adequate to satisfy all human or ecosystem requirements.

2. CAN WATER BE RECYCLED?
Water recycles itself naturally. Heat causes water to evaporate as moisture into the sky. It cools and forms rains, which comes back to Earth. It is also possible for us to recycle water. For example, water from bathrooms can be reused to flush toilets.

3. WHAT IS WATER POLLUTION?
Water gets polluted when material such as garbage, sewage, industrial wastes is discharged in it. Pollutants such as the ones described above do not belong in the water and their presence change the conditions in the water environment. These changes cause damage to all animals, plants and people who depend on the water to survive.

4. HOW DOES WATER BECOME CONTAMINATED?

The common causes of water contamination are from what we call "surface run-off" or from direct discharges. In the case of surface run-off, when rain falls, the water runs off on the surface of the Earth. If this water runs through human and animal faeces and sewage, it carries with it bacteria and germs into streams, rivers, ponds, dams, and lakes. This is often the case where toilets are lacking, inadequate or are poorly constructed.

Direct discharges include the discharge of sewage and industrial waste through pipes into rivers and lakes. It is from bathing in or drinking such water that the bacteria and germs enter our bodies. Agricultural practices also contribute to contamination of groundwater and rivers. Many farmers use pesticides to kill destructive insects and fertilisers to improve their production. When it rains, these compounds can easily end up in the run-off and contaminate the water bodies.

5. IS IT TRUE THAT WATER KILLS?

This is not true. Yes, you could drown in a river or a swimming pool. But most water-related deaths are not directly caused by water itself. Contaminated water or diseases where water is the key vector are responsible for the majority of the deaths, especially amongst young children. Such diseases are known as waterborne diseases.

6. WHAT IS ACID RAIN?

As the name suggests, acid rain is rain which is acidic. The rain becomes acidic when gases in the air dissolve in the rainwater and form various acids. Sulphur dioxide (SO_2) and nitrogen oxides (NO_x) are the main causes of acid rain. Factories are significant sources of air pollution. Acid deposition has a variety of effects, including damage to forests, soils and buildings. Acid rain also reduces how far and clearly we can see through the air, an effect called visibility reduction.

Another dangerous compound emitted by many factories is mercury. Mercury in water can easily find its way into human beings through fish or drinking water. Mercury poisoning is very dangerous to humans, especially to women and children.

7. IS GROUNDWATER INEXHAUSTIBLE?

No, the amount of groundwater is limited. When overdrawn, the level decreases so that you have to dig deeper to get water or water is not accessible in practical terms. This is already a problem in the Arabian Peninsula, China, India, Mexico, Russia and the United States where the volumes of water being withdrawn is far in excess of natural recharge rates.

8. WHAT IS SALINIZATION?

Salinization refers to increased salt concentration in soils. This occurs when saline (salty) water is used for irrigation. In areas where water quickly evaporates the salt is accumulated in the topsoil. Salinization makes the soil unfit for agricultural purposes because most crops cannot survive in excessively salty environments.

The term salinization is also used to describe the process where freshwater sources come in contact with saltwater. This can occur if for example the sea level rises and allows seawater to permeate groundwater sources.

9. WHAT IS DESALINATION?

Desalination is the process of removing the salt from salty water such as seawater. When salt is removed, the water can be used for drinking. The process of desalination is still costly but as new technologies are being developed the costs are declining and the use of desalination for additional supply of freshwater may be feasible in the future. Today, the most important users of desalination plants are the countries in the Near East.

10. WHAT IS THE RELATIONSHIP BETWEEN FOREST COVER AND WATER?

Trees and other vegetation are very important. When rain falls on bare ground the surface run-off is faster so less water is retained and floods and erosion are more likely to occur. Where there is forest cover water run-off is slowed down allowing more to seep into the ground.

11. HOW IS WATER MADE SAFE FOR DRINKING?

There are several ways in which water is made safe for drinking. These methods include:

- Boiling - The easiest method is to boil the water. This kills bacteria and germs. It is important to store the water in a clean vessel, which should be covered. It is also important to be aware that contamination can also take place in the house. For instance, it is not good practice to draw water from a vessel by dipping into it. Instead, pouring out is recommended.

- Filtration - Filtration is another method; but it is important that the filter is effective. If in doubt water should be boiled as well. Large treatment plants often first filter water before chemicals are applied to remove dissolved compounds and kill germs.

- Use of chemicals - Chemicals such as chlorine can be added to water either to kill germs or to remove dissolved compounds. The compounds are removed when the chemicals bind to the dissolved matter and make it sink to the bottom. This process is called flocculation or coagulation.

12. CAN RAINWATER BE USED FOR DRINKING?

Collecting rainwater is also called rainwater harvesting. Rainwater can easily provide safe drinking water in most parts of the world, where air pollution is minimal.

13. HOW MUCH WATER DOES AN AVERAGE PERSON USE PER DAY?

In developed countries one person uses about 230 litres (50 gallons) of water per day. A modern water bathtub takes about 100-150 litres of water. This can be compared to some countries in Africa and Asia where a family of eight uses only 20 litres per day. Taking a shower instead of a bath takes less than a third of the amount of water. Household demand for water is rising particularly among the wealthy consumers in both developed and developing countries. It seems as if when the standard of living improves people tend to consume more water.

14. IS IT TRUE THAT SOME PEOPLE FIGHT OVER WATER?

Communities have fought over water resources, for example over water holes in semi-arid areas. Since more and more people are subject to water stress the potential for conflicts over water resources is increasing. However, since rivers and other water sources are often shared between two or more countries, water has also been an important reason for good cooperation between countries.

15. DO PEOPLE IN URBAN AREAS EXPERIENCE LACK OF ACCESS TO DRINKING WATER?

Although we tend to associate urban areas with improved services, cities in developing countries still face acute water shortages. The situation is worse in low-cost residential areas as well as in the informal (slum) settlements.

List of
contributing
children
Chapter 9

List of contributing schools and children

Many children from all over the world contributed to this book by sending us drawings, photos, paintings, poems and stories. The number of entries received was overwhelming. We thank all children, teachers and all those who assisted them to think through the theme on water. It was not possible to use all the entries. However, we acknowledge with gratitude each of you for sending in your contributions. Below is a list of the schools and children who had contributed with their work by the time the book was being compiled. From UNEP, we say a big THANK YOU to all of you!

BRUNEI
Dk Musfirah Wajihah Binti Pengiran Haji Zainurin

BULGARIA
Michail Lakatnick Primary School
Mihail Kalchev

Peter Beron Primary School
Atanas Kostadinov

Peyo Yavorov School
Dion Nikolaev Nikolov
Kolev Hristov

Pinokio Kindergarten
Dima Tsvetanova
Plamena Nedialkova
Vesselina Karaivanova

Detelina Kindergarten
Dobrudja Technical School
Kiril and Metodi School
Petko Rachev Slaveikov Primary School
Vasil Aprilov School
Vulshebstvo Kindergarten

CHINA
Zhang Jiaxin
Yao Momo
Mo Chen
Liang Jiaxin

CROATIA
Augusta Cesarca Primary School
Margerita Ramljak

Vladimir Gortan Primary School
Ana Sokolic
Angela Karacic
Damir Molnar
Hrvoje Horvat
Ivan Lubina
Jelena Simic
Paula Grskovic

Nova Gradiska Secondary School
Maric Igor
Martina Jugovic

Voltino Primary School
Vjekoslav Parac Primary School

CYPRUS
B' Elementary of Ypsonas
Yiota Hadjilouka

B' Elementary School Kato Polemidion

ESTONIA
Ala Basic School

FINLAND
Kevätkummun koulu
Katri Lahti
Juho Hänninem
Paula ja Rosa

Kinnarin koulu

GREECE
13th & 21st Primary Schools of Keratsini

HONG KONG
Cheng Lut Ming
Lo Wing Tung
Kwok Yen Yi, Estee
Lee Cheuk Tat
Yuen Ka Hei, Cathy
Lin Hiu See, Jessie
Leung Wing Yu
Wong Wai, Flona
Chau Ching Li, Jenny

INDIA
G. Reinu Shyle
Madhura Y. Herekar
Mayur S. Gahiwad
Neha Sanjay Vavle
Rijma Noor Sayyad
A. Siji
Radhika Bharathi

INDONESIA
Grace F. Candra
Evelyn L. Wijaya
Ivan Aris Nugroho

IRELAND
Ballinderreen National School
Sarah Herbert

Ballyglass National School
Myles Higgins
Shane Bermingham

St. Joseph's Boys National School
Aaron
Alex Reid
Brian
David Tracey
Jack McGarry
Liam O'Neill

ITALY

Carchidio Faenza Primary School
Scuola Elementare di Orbetello Scalo
Scuola Dell'infanzia Via Mazzini
Scuole Benedettine della Provvidenza
Primary School
Scuola Elementare Giovanni Xxiii

KENYA

Kisumu Junior Academy
Oshwal Academy
Premier Academy
The Banda School
Ikonzo Primary School
Makini School
Central Primary School
Achuth Primary School
Peace Junior Academy
Muhito Primary School
Melvin Jones Lions Academy
Loreto Msongari
SCLP Samaj
Malezi School
Muslim Girls Primary
Loreto Conv. Msongari
Arya Vedic School
Baraka Primary School
Aga Khan Primary
Light Academy

Kisumu Senior Academy
Surinder Roopra
Mansi Kotak

Chavakali High School
Chiluyi Byron
Thomas Imboywa
DeClerk Mon'gare
Victor Andani
Erick Machuki
Maurice Rono
Shadrack Adoyo
Daniel Ambembo
Johnson Muhando
Najoli Benjamin
Mark Kipkoech
Bernard Sabwa
Bruno Okoth
Mark Kipkoech
Alloys Inagwe

Bware Secondary School
Madegwa Godfrey
Oban'ga Kennedy
Reuben Mugasu
Faith Nagweya
Lucas Otieno
Danga Julius
Yvonne Ayayo
Geoffrey Omogo
Samuel Gavo

Lunira Nelson
Sarah Achieng
Rose Okach
David Kagali
Msibega Lucy A.
Alex Otieno
Achieng Olwen
Ayayo Sylphano
Otieno G. Phillip

Wanjohi Girls Secondary School
Veronicah Mburu
Mary W. Njoroge
Josephine Njoroge
Mary Wambugu,
Oshwal Academy
Viraaj Malde

Oshwal High School
Vishal Shah
Bhavin Girishbhai Patel
Mansukh D. Valeria
Hiren Jayraj Vara
Harshil Mahesh Shah

C.G.H.U. Secondary School
Manpreet Kaur Bahra
Maheshwari Andhavarafu

Nilam Patel, C.G.H.U. Sec. School
Jyoti H. Parmar

La Verne School
Botany C. Peter

Peponi Secondary School
Chris Hemphill
Grace Mwangi
Jessica Behrens
Laura J. Kiplagat
Michael Zhao
Aupal Patel
Jackson D. Makangara

IFO Secondary School
Johnson Opira Okello

Ulanda Girls High School
Maureen A. Onyango
Hellen Adul

Daghaley Secondary School
Mohamed Suleiman M
Ahmed Muktar Abdi
Mohamed Ali Ahmed
Alrahman Ibrahim Abdi
Abdirahman Ibrahim Abdi
Ali Mohamud Farah

Ofafa Jericho High
Henry Mugo Maina
Peter Mburu
John Kangethe

Carmel Girls Secondary
Eunice Wanjiku
Shalotte Salmi Otieno
Doreen Ivy Adhiambo

Alliance High School
Michael Mokaya
Andrew Amayo
Muthiga G. Michael
Malezi School
Mark Ondicho,
Thiodore Kiyaka

Kenya High School
Nancy Adera

Buruburu Girls Secondary School
Lorna W. Maseghe

Loreto Conv. Msongari
Wavinya Maliti Susan
Stephanie Mwaura
Veronica Njeri Karanja

Arya Vedic School
Vandana Pali
Riddhi Patel

MEXICO

Angel Matute Vidal
Luis Erick
Luz Mariana
Luisa Fernanda
Armando Valdez Mandujana
Uriel Pina Valdes
Bergona Erdozain
Andrea Alfarez
Martinez Dazquez
Jimena Gorostizaga
Andrea Montezebe
Cada Dia Quedame
Marimar Carrasco
Dean Mari
Hector Coompo
Samtiago Soto
Bruno Frigo
Jose Gorostiza
Nick Sondo
Fatima Alvarez
Diego Del Rio
Pada Rolama
Mayte de Arino
Jose Ignacio

Mira Flores
Anna Maria Olavari
Alejandra de la Cruz
Mariamar Lamas
Santiago Alfonso Galeano
Monitel Fernandez
Mariana Zinseo
Siyyet Chendran
Jamie Lee
Bagona Rodriquez
Alberto Vargas Alonso
Lucrecia Loyo
Santiago
Maria Fenanda
Sofia Lomeli
Raphael Diez
Gonzalo Anton Tazcon
Astefania May
Christianne Sammaan
Angel Matute Vidal
Alejandra Sandaval
Alma Gabriela
Karina Ayala
Blanca Estella
Daniel Ordonez
Alberto B Yanez
Daniela Mandujano

Brian Avilla Ordonez
Alberto Bravo
Albero Martiney
Erica Saucedo
Alfredo Mucio
Liz Mari
Lucia Taboada
Alenjandra
Fenanda Catallisto

Leandra Rosado
Carolina Pimienta
Jesus Abraham
Maria Zua
Maria Fernanda
Christian Joanan
Anna Karen
Amaranta Galicia
Quetzalli Zamudio
Laura Bautista
Jaqueline Mucio
Daryel Jared
Erick Flores
Maria Fernanda
Paola Mirelle
Gomey Alejandro
Martha Bahena
Dominique Alcantara

Hebreo Sefaradi
Lilliana Garcia
Alan Guerson
Ariela Schmidt
Pepe Capuano
Itai Nedvedovich
Vicky Mitrani
Daniella Nisenbaum
Marcos Cohen
Reina Farji
Samuel Cohen
Yasef Haras
Janet Michel
Batia Poyastro
Alliya Brzezinski
Ariela Wolcovich
Sharon Israel
Gloria Saba
Simon Klach
Milton Olsoff
David Benguitat
Sharon Fainstein
Orit Yedid
Michel Yedid
Jacobo Motola
Daniel Sarfati Weitzner
Tamara Braverman
Jose Antonio de Miguel
Millie Bistre Varon
Kenia Valderrama
Aura Selene Ruiz
Fernanda Arechavaleta
Diego Gutierrez
Victor Ramirez
Nicola Garcia
Tania Tovac
Miniva Barriera
Daniela Ducoing

Kenya Estrada
Fernando Rodriguez
Myrna Macedo
Luisa Arenal
Daniela Nava Ducoing
Antonio Miguel
Jorge Zamora
Dzoala Castillo
Rafael Oliveras
Yael Francisco
Elida Barroeta
Myrna macedo
Mayra Ugalde
Lesley Reyes
Lousa Arenal
Fernando Gutierrez
Mellisa Gonzalez
Gabriel Garcia
Karen Velazquez
Mariana Gonzalez
Michael Cohen
Vivian Bialostozky
Alicia Masliah
Albert Abouaf
Alinjandro Broid
David Kenazi
Galia Matatoff
Mike Braverman
Salvador Sevilla
Jenny Motola Stern
Albert Alfille Abouaf
Denise Rosental Wachnowetzky
Lillian Sevilla

MYANMAR
Mg Zin Ko Ko
Mg Aung Kyaw Hein
May Htoo Myat Mon
Ma Hnin Fi Ei Phwe

NEPAL
Riji Shrestha Khanal

PORTUGAL
EB1 de Adães
José Fabrica
Rui Pedro

EB1 de Gouvães da Serra
Beatriz
Belém
Bruno
Félix
Patrícia
Pedro
Rafaela

EB1 de São Martinho do Bispo
Ana Rita
Hugo
Luis Banaco
Maria Francisca
Rolende Mendes
Tiago Marques
1st grade students
3rd grade students
4th grade students

EBI de Santa Catarina
Ana Pereira
Juliana Costa

EB1 de Paço
EB1 do Alquebre

REPUBLIC OF KOREA
Ha Jeong, Kim
Ye Na Lee

SEYCHELLES
Anse Boileau Secondary School
Nelcia Kilindo
Malshini Senaratne

Anse Rozale School
Jonathan Azemia

Glacis School
Fritznel Cupidon
Jean-Yoes Marie
Mario Simara
Marcia Servina
Vanessa Bastienne
La Retraite School
Hawksbill Wildlife Club

Bel ean School
Ginat Vidot
Julie Tyrant

International School
Alvine Gabribl
Zhuoyu Wei
Lucas D'offaz
Alessandro Marzocchi
RenePierre Alis
Marcus Fanny
Monique Fourie
Nadine Colin
Stephanie Padazachy
Gary Michell
Jean Marc Prea
Srinivsan Pillay
Claire Ormshaw
KyleThompson
Ilma Ali
Cathy Jiang
Ania Pool
Snigdha

SLOVENIA
Aleksandra Sauperl
Janja Miljus
Janka Padeznika
Marko Burjek
Melisa Zilic

Lenart Primary School
Grega Markus

Dragatus Primary School
France Preseren Elementary School
"8 Talcev" Logatec Primary School
Miran Jarc Primary School
Primoza Tru Barja
Radenci Primary School
Smarjeta Primary School
Tabor II Primary School
Zrece Primary School

SOUTH AFRICA
Makone Vincent Mohan
Mpumalanga
Dwaf Kimberley
Mmammakatse

Water World
Chapter 5
List of contributing children
An educational booklet on water
85

Tdyoki Public School
Nelisa Meutyana

Matswathaka primary School
J M, Ndindwa High School
Sol Plaatjie Secondary School
Veyukhono Secondary School

SPAIN
I.E.S Maria Zambrano
Keisla Alvarez Abreu
Lara Calderon Calderon
Irene Casado Navarro
Almudena Esteban Abengozar
Noelia Garcia de Castro
Carmen Jimenez Jimenez
Ana Jimenez Jimenez
Isabel Lopez Tejedor

CP Nuestra Señora de la Presentación

SRI LANKA
Nithiyanantha Kurinchikumaran
Lakshika Chamini Weragoda

THAILAND
Pornchanok Rattanasarun

UGANDA
Buligo Primary school
Raziya Asuman
Mutesi Babra
Sharifa Mohammed
Kintu Peter
Dembula Herbert
Mpata Herman
Magumba Jerome
Bakaki Denis
Makhendo Boniface

Triangle Secondary School
Kintu Anthony
Kyaterekera Abou Karimi

Valley Hill School
Deeba Julius
Mwesigila Richard
Waiswa Tadeo
Gaifuba Isaac
Muwanga Isaac
Bategeera Esther
Ibanda Ronald
Tenywa Joel
Wanyirwa Paul
Kalimwigi David
Kibaale Mohammed
Sseguza Francis
Kamaga Minsaki
Taze James
Wakibi Samson
Wagubi Marsden

P.M.M. Girls School
Nangobi Rita
Adongo Kristabelle
Nabiriye Christine
Nabiriye Caroline
Babuleka Dorothy
Mukhwala Elsie
Naikazi Grace
Amina Abubaker

Kyomugisha Christine
Pipino Sandra
Akello Gladys Gillian

Mt. St. Mary's School, Namagunga
Kediini Jonah
Batte Juliana
Alal B Sophie

Buluba Primary School
Adong Immaculate
Babeyo Shafiq
Aplo Catherine

Gulu Public School
Ibrahim Sharifa
Acen Clare
Apiyo Edna
Ochaka Hendry
Komakech David

Gulu Secondary School
Babra Layet
Ojara Emmanuel
Obali Okema
Odongo Johnson
Opira Raphael
Apiyo Susan
Ajok Jackline
Okello Deogracious
Nokra Felix
Tabu Patrick
Olara Morish
Kilama Bosco
Okelo Denis
Okumu Peter
Moris Drogocan
Opiro Kenneth
Oryema Tommy

Koro Abili Primary School
Ocira Richard
Okello Richard
Ojok Grant
Adong Jovanna
Amony Julie
Justine Mwaka
Richard Benjamin
Okoy Richard
Oliver Ojok
Opiyo John
Obita Benjamin

Bishop Angelo Negri Primary School
Likwiya Johnson
Onen George William
Okot Piero
Oketayot Stephen

Sir Samuel Baker School
Omony Holy Geoffrey

Orawa Primary School
Aziku John
Sunday Monica
Draru Lilian
Bileru Harriet

Awaru Jenety
Siasa Ramadan
Swali Dudu
Mila Motema
Stephen Orawa
Adukule Francis
Abele Stephen
Adomati Alex
Night Lillian
Tallibo Margaret
Asuna Peace

Ociba Primary School
Achori Stephen Droti
Edeku Tom
Amati Kennedy
Abdalla Dusman Gadafi
Adiru Margaret
Anguzu Moab
Ondoru Flavia
Medina Andama
Adriko Bob
Achidri Stephen
Adrole Samuel

UNITED KINGDOM
Ashley School
Gemma Smith
Laura Flanagan
Nicola Jordan
Stevie Corry

Belgrave Infant School
James Wither
Alexander McNee

Canon Burrows C of E Primary School
Alex Heaton
Alicia Warner
Andrew Montana
Bilal Majed
Hannah Sharrock
Nathan Greenough
Summer Lynn

Dunfane School
Gary Hill
Christopher Parkhill
Ryan Ormandy
Joseph Canavan

Sir Alexander Fleming Primary School
Anton Davidson
Bethany Nenshi
Callum George
Charlene Medlicott
Codey Parkes
Connor F.
Daniel Will
Elizabeth Kelly
Hannah Lister
Jamie Bright
Lauren Baldi
Lisa Simpkins
Mundeep Kaur
Nicky Butler

Sarah Clarke
Sophie Chamberlain
Tara Ellis-Jeffries

Raglan Primary School
Andrico Karoulla
Ghaffar Moten
Isobel Scott
Laureen Dumper
Maliha Moten

St Leonard's CE Primary School
Amanda Moulton
Rebecca Heffernan
Zoë Price

Stanborough School
Paul Ogbuigwe

Weston Coyney Junior School
Abigail Irwin
Elleanor Tunstall
Jessica Bailey
Kimberley Gouldsmith
Laura Boon
Laura Morgan
Liam Burbidge
Nicole Dean
Nicole Smith
Ryan Thorley
Sam Heath
Stacey Brown
Stacey Townsend
Tim Jenkinson
Tyler Edwards

Lunnasting Primary School

VANUATU
Sainimilli Toara
Erique Karlzau
Yasmine Kamasteia
Judy Jack
Alwed E. Courhney

Please get back to us!

We would very much appreciate if you would contact us after reading this booklet. No matter whether you are a child or an adult your comments on the booklet are valuable to us. Please send us an e-mail or an ordinary letter and indicate how you came in contact with the booklet and how you found it. We look forward to your mails!

Head, Environmental Education and Training Unit
Division of Environmental Policy Implementation
UNEP
P.O. Box 30552
Nairobi, Kenya

env.edu@unep.org

TUNZA means "treat with care and affection" in the Kiswahili language of Kenya, where UNEP's international headquarters are based. Further information about UNEP's TUNZA Children and Youth programme is available from:

Head, Children and Youth Unit
Division of Communications and Public Information
UNEP
P.O. Box 30552
Nairobi, Kenya

@

children.youth@unep.org